The Aquinas Lecture, 1971

REASON AND FAITH REVISITED

Under the auspices of the
Wisconsin-Alpha Chapter of Phi Sigma Tau

By

FRANCIS H. PARKER, Ph.D.

MARQUETTE UNIVERSITY PRESS
MILWAUKEE
1971

Library of Congress Catalog Number: 79-154285

To Henry John Schriber

and

Marion Thelma Winegard Schriber

Prefatory

The Wisconsin-Alpha Chapter of Phi
Sigma Tau, the National Honor Society
for Philosophy at Marquette University,
each year invites a scholar to deliver a
lecture in honor of St. Thomas Aquinas,
whose feast day formerly was March 7.
The lectures are customarily given on the
first Sunday of March. The 1971 Aquinas
Lecture *Reason and Faith Revisited* was
delivered on March 7 in Todd Wehr
Chemistry by Professor Francis H. Parker,
Head of the Philosophy Department, Purdue University.

Professor Parker was born June 23,
1920, in Kuala Lumpur, Malaysia. He
earned his A.B. in 1941 at Evansville (Ind.)
College, his M.A. in 1947 at Indiana University, and his Ph.D. in 1949 at Harvard
University.

He began his teaching career as a
teaching fellow at Harvard. In 1949 he
joined the faculty of Haverford College,
where he became a full Professor in 1961
and chairman of the department of philo-

sophy from 1963-1966. In 1966 he became the head of the philosophy department at Purdue University.

Professor Parker has had a continuing interest in the philosophical problems connected with human knowledge, both in its logical and its epistemological aspects. He has also written extensively in the area of the philosophy of religion.

The publications of Professor Parker include: *Logic as a Human Instrument* (with Prof. H. B. Veatch), New York: Harper, 1959; *The Story of Western Philosophy*, Bloomington: Indiana University Press, 1967; articles in two encyclopedias and many articles in philosophical journals. To these publications Phi Sigma Tau is pleased to add: *Reason and Faith Revisited*.

Reason and Faith Revisited

My title is deliberately ambiguous, for in this lecture I want to do two different but related things. In the first place, I want to attempt an analysis of the nature of reason and of faith and of the relationship between them, and in this respect I want to revisit an age when this problem was thought to be more important than it apparently is today. In the second place, I want to advocate the acceptance of both reason and faith, as they will here be analyzed; and in this way too I want to return to an age when such dual acceptance was more popular than it seems to me to be today. This joint project I hope will be appropriate in a lecture meant to honor St. Thomas Aquinas, since I take him to be the greatest synthesizer of reason and faith and the greatest advocate of both of them as united that the western world has known. It should be confessed, however,

that a complete return to the age of Aquinas is today impossible, at least for me.
Much as I prize, even envy, St. Thomas'
synthesis, too much water has gone over
the falls of modernity for us to be able to
return it all to its original reservoir. Or as
Thomas Wolfe wrote, to change the meta-
phor, "You can't go home again." A visit
back home may be possible, however, even
if one has changed too much to live there
again permanently. This, then, is what I
hope for in this lecture. I want to try to be
a medieval in advocating both reason and
faith and their synthesis; but my concep-
tions of reason and faith and their relationship, and my reasons for advocating them,
will be seen to be influenced—some may
say infected — by the modern thought
which I (and, indeed, all of us) have in-
herited. Let us now proceed.

I

Let us look first at the position of reason or intellect, let us look at the stand of
the rationalist. For the rationalist nothing
is taken on faith; nothing is taken for granted (nothing is taken for "granite," one of

my students once wrote). Things are accepted only when they are rationally or intellectually seen to be so. This rational or intellectual seeing need not be as narrow as the so-called "continental rationalists" insisted that it should be, however. The rationalist I am referring to is just the rational or reasonable man of everyday life—the rationalist in the general and popular sense of that term. He is the man who believes only on the basis of evidence—either his own personal experience or else his rational inferences from his own personal experience. For the rational man, then, believing means seeing (or hearing or touching, etc.) or a rational inference from hearing or seeing, and so forth. Or at least he holds that believing *ought* to mean experiencing or inferring from experiencing. The rational man may of course recognize that in a moment of weakness he may believe without having the relevant experience or rational inferences from experience; but he holds that he ought not to do this, and he recognizes this as a flaw in his character.

Hence for the rationalist here considered a belief is to be accepted when and only when it is rational in the sense that it satisfies one or the other of the following two conditions: First, the belief to be accepted must seem to be a record of immediate experience; for example, "This is paper before me." Beliefs of this kind let us call *"first order beliefs."* Or, second, the belief to be accepted must seem to follow from some other one of the believer's beliefs by logical rules; for example, "April will be warmer than March (in the northern hemisphere)." Beliefs of this kind let us call *"second order beliefs."* Let me now try to explain first and second order beliefs more fully.

First of all, I want to use the expressions "immediate experience" and "logical rules" quite broadly. The immediate experience seemingly recorded in a first order belief is usually sensory; but it need not be and sometimes it is not, as we shall see. It could be an extra-sensory perception or a super-sensory experience, but it must at least always be an immediate and personal experience. In like manner I mean logical rules in the broad sense in which they are utilized and concretely recognized in common life and in which they are approximately codified by philosophers of ordinary life and language. Thus, while these logical rules are usually the deductive and inductive ones of the textbooks, they are sometimes more special ones such as those of law, of love, of religion, and of war. They must, however, be *logical* rules and not merely psychological generalizations, for I am here concerned with what *ought* to be believed and not merely with what *happens* to be believed. Yet it is not my present purpose to define or codify logical rules or immediate experiences, and I will be satisfied to count as such whatever people would ordinarily so count. All I here want to do is to define the stance of the rationalist as that of one who regards a belief as acceptable when and only when it seems to be a record of immediate experience (a first order belief) or seems to follow by logical rules from some other of that believer's beliefs (a second order belief)— whatever ordinary people and philoso-

phers may decide to let count as an immediate experience or as a logical rule.

Now another caveat is indicated. To
say that a belief is a first order one or a
second order one, or to say that a first order or a second order belief is or ought to
be *accepted,* is not to say that that belief
is *true.* Please note that I said that a first
order belief is one that *seems* to be a record of immediate experience and that a
second order belief is one that *seems* to
follow from some other accepted belief—
not that either must actually be what it
seems to be. As a matter of fact, even if
the first order belief really were a record
of immediate experience as well as seeming to be, or even if the second order
belief really did follow from some other
accepted belief by logical rules as well as
seeming to do so, it would not yet quite
follow that these beliefs are thereby true.
In order for this to follow we would need
some additional premises such as that "Immediate experience is veracious" and that
"Whatever is logical is true." Premises of

this second type I will shortly consider as "third order beliefs."

All this is just to say that it is sometimes rational to accept a belief which is as a matter of fact false (though of course it is not rational—or even possible—to accept a belief which one *believes* to be false). April might one year be colder than March; but, in the absence of contrary evidence, it is rational to believe that April will be warmer than March. A physician may possibly be wrong in his diagnosis, but on the basis of the evidence available to him it is rational for him to accept that diagnosis. Thus I am not now talking about the truth or falsity of beliefs but rather about their rationality. If it makes the matter clearer, one may put it in terms of the truth-value of a proposition (for instance, that "April will be warmer than March") in distinction from the rationality of a belief in that proposition, or a belief that that proposition is true. Once more, it is only the rationality of the belief in a proposition or that a proposition is true that I am here concerned with, not with the truth of the proposition itself.

Since most beliefs are second order ones, let us consider first what is involved in second order belief. A second order belief is accepted because it seems to follow from some other accepted belief (by logical rules, deductive or inductive, etc.). But what is the reason for accepting this *other* belief? Well, sometimes this other belief is a first order belief, a belief which seems to be a record of immediate experience. Or sometimes this other belief seems to follow from a first order belief. Often, however, the ground on which the second order belief is accepted is some other belief which is derived from some other belief which is derived from some other belief, etc., etc., with no final grounding in any first order belief. This is to say that second order beliefs often rest on beliefs which are not proven and are not records of immediate experience and which are therefore not rational in the defined sense. But this seems to make rationalism turn into its opposite: for the rationalist every belief must either be proven or be based on experience, but some of the proven ones require acceptance of beliefs which are neither proven nor based on experience. Let us call these latter beliefs *"third order beliefs"*: beliefs which are presupposed by second order beliefs but which are themselves neither proven nor records of experience. A third order belief, then, is a belief which is necessary as a premise for a second order belief but which is itself neither a second order nor a first order belief.

Now third order beliefs look very much like articles of faith—since they are necessary as premises for second order beliefs while not being themselves rational in the defined sense, since, that is, they are neither first order nor second order beliefs. Hence supposedly rational beliefs seem to rest necessarily upon faith, and the thesis that this is always and necessarily so has become quite popular in certain circles in recent times. Note, for example, Henry Margenau's claim that faith is the foundation of science itself—that supposed bastion of rationality:

. . . all physical explanation starts with premises, *i.e.*, postulates, and not with proven
truths. In the old days, these postulates
were regarded as axioms, that is, as propositions which are self-evident and indubi-
tably true. This view has now been abandoned by almost all scientists, who look
upon their postulates as tentative starting
points for theoretical deductions, the evidence or truth of which increases with
confirmation of their specific consequences.

. . . even so fundamental a discipline
as arithmetic has its own limited range of
application, and . . . its truth is contingent
upon the acceptance of certain premises
called postulates which, by virtue of their
generality and our familiarity with them,
frequently take on the semblance of self-
evidence.

Because of this logical structure, because of its need for fundamental postula-
tional commitments, science here joins two
other areas of human concern, religion and
ethics. The basic assumptions are called
faith in religion, *ideals* or *norms* in ethics;
in science they go by the prosaic name of
axioms or *postulates*. The scientific equiva-
lent to the act of faith in religion, the act
of dedication to an ideal in ethics, is the
acceptance of basic postulates.

... Items of faith, whether they belong
to religion, the field of action or understanding, form anchors for the ships of our
lives, and science is no exception to this
general rule.[1]

At one level Margenau is surely wrong
in contending that science rests on postulates accepted merely on faith. Margenau
himself notes in the above quotation that
"the evidence or truth of [these alleged
postulates] increases with confirmation of
their specific consequences," but this exactly means that these supposed postulates
are not accepted merely on faith. The alleged postulates or axioms of science are
not really articles of faith at all because
they are *proven* (though not conclusively)
by experience and logic, or else scientists
abandon them for other and different "postulates." Hence these alleged articles of
scientific faith follow from other beliefs,
and ultimately from first order beliefs or
experience. Thus they cannot really be articles of faith. As a matter of fact, they are
not even postulates or axioms in the stricter
sense given these terms in axiomatic sys-

tems, because the truth-value (if any) of
genuine postulates or axioms is independ-
ent of their logical consequences whereas
the truth of Margenau's supposed postulates or axioms depends on their logical
consequences. What Margenau calls axioms or postulates may perhaps best be
called hypotheses, but whatever they are
called they are certainly not articles of
faith. They are rather entirely rational in
the ordinary sense which I have defined.

At a deeper level Margenau has an important point, however. Granting that science is rational in our defined sense by
virtue of the fact that it regards as unac-
ceptable all beliefs which are inconsistent
with experience or with other accepted
scientific beliefs, this attitude, to be justifiable, must presuppose the more fundamental belief that "truth is consistent,"
both with itself and with experience. But
this presupposed belief that "truth is consistent" is not rational in the defined sense.
In the first place, the belief that truth is
consistent is apparently not a second order
belief—that is, it is not derivable from any

other belief — for a demonstration of it would beg the question by presupposing that truth is consistent. This is so because by a demonstrated proposition we mean one that ought not in consistency to be false since certain other propositions (called premises) are true—and in the case of deductive demonstration or strict proof we mean by a demonstrated proposition one that *must* not or *can* not consistently be false since the premises are true.

In the second place, it does not seem plausible to hold that the belief that truth is consistent—that is, that *all* truth whatever is *necessarily* consistent—is a first order belief, a report of immediate experience, in any concrete and specific sense of "experience," since this belief is too abstract and general and has too much universality and necessity to be captured in any single concrete and specific experience. On the contrary, an "experience" which could be this universal and necessary would have to be much more abstract and conceptual than what is normally termed an experience. One may of course call the apprehension of the consistency of all truth, or of the proposition that truth is consistent, an experience if one so wishes. If so, however, it must surely be granted that it is a very different kind of experience with a very different kind of object than the immediate personal experience and its object which are ostensibly recorded in what I have called a first order belief.

In a first order belief the ostensibly recorded object is some restricted part of reality—for example, this paper—so what is apparently recorded about it is not necessarily true of all reality. In a belief such as that all truth whatsoever is necessarily consistent, however, the recorded object of the awareness or experience is unrestricted and absolutely universal—for example, being—so that what is recorded about it is necessarily true of all reality such that there is no possibility of an exception. Truth is therefore a transcendental, a property of being as such which therefore transcends all differences. What is true of being as such must be true of every possible particular being. But the converse is not the case. What is true of some particular being —say this paper—need not be true of other beings or of being as such. What is regarded as an experience ordinarily is always of such a particular being, though there are thinkers who claim that there is an experience or intuition of being as such.[2] I have no objection to this so long as this type of experience is sharply distinguished from the type of experience apparently recorded in what I am calling a first order belief, even though I prefer to use some other term such as intellectual insight or intuitive reason.[3]

Hence the belief that truth is consistent is neither a second order nor a first order belief, and it is therefore not rational in the defined sense. And yet this belief that truth is consistent is necessary to the very meaning of second order belief— defined as that which seems to follow (by logical rules) from some other accepted belief—and thus also necessary to rationalism as defined. And this is very probably true also of some other beliefs in addition to the belief that truth is consistent.

Putting this point more abstractly, you believe that *p* because you believe that *q* and because you believe that *p* follows from *q* (by logical rules). But this complex fact is not a *reason* for believing that *p* unless you also believe three other propositions: (1) Whatever follows from another belief *should* be believed. (2) Whatever does not follow from another belief *need not* be believed. (3) Whatever contradicts or is inconsistent with another belief *should not* be believed (*must* not be believed when the contradicted belief has been demonstrated or strictly proven—that is, has been deduced from true premises). But these three beliefs are *third* order ones and are therefore not rational in the defined sense; they are not records of immediate experience and they do not follow by logical rules from other accepted beliefs. Yet they are absolutely necessary to second order beliefs and therefore also to rationalism as defined.

If some one were now to claim that these three beliefs do indeed follow from other accepted beliefs, then what I am now

saying would simply be true of those other
accepted beliefs from which my three are
claimed to follow. Or if, again, those *other*
accepted beliefs were in turn claimed to be
derivable, then what I am now saying
would simply be true of whatever beliefs
would be taken to be first premises. And
of course some beliefs or others would
have to be taken as first premises; one must
start somewhere. In any case, therefore,
second order beliefs require other beliefs
which are neither second order nor first
order ones.

So here, at a deeper level, Margenau's
thesis contains a truth: rational enterprises,
even the sciences, rest on beliefs which are
not rational in the sense intended within
those enterprises. Let us use the term
"principles" to refer to these apparently
non-rational beliefs which are presupposed
by rational beliefs as we have defined
them, and by the "rational" enterprises
they compose. Principles, then, are those
third order beliefs which are presupposed
by or are necessary to second order beliefs.
Now the question again rises, but this time

more specifically and fundamentally: Are
principles articles of faith? Must principles
be accepted on faith?

II

Principles are certainly like articles of
faith in two respects: they are underivable,
and they are also foundational. That principles are underivable and foundational we
have just seen. That articles of faith are
underivable seems obvious, for if they
were derivable (by logical rules) we
would call them rational inferences rather
than articles of faith. That they are also
foundational follows from their underiva-
bility so long as other beliefs are derived
from them; and this certainly seems to be
true of at least most of the major revealed
tenets of the great western religions—for
example, the incarnation of God in Jesus.
From this belief may be derived, for instance, the belief in the infallible authority
of Jesus. Furthermore, it is very tempting
to regard principles as articles of faith because this yields the comforting position
which Margenau espouses. It solves the
problem of the relation of science and re-

ligion and the problem of the relation of
fact and value by grounding them all on
faith—albeit on different kinds of faith. It
permits us to say that everyone has a faith
—indeed that everyone *must* have a faith—
and this puts us all in the same boat.

Yet in another and very important way
principles are also quite unlike articles of
faith. Principles can be *seen* (intellectually) to be necessarily true, whereas articles
of faith can not be; "faith is the evidence
of things *not* seen." This of course does not
mean that principles are always and by
everyone seen to be necessarily true, any
more than it means that everyone accepts
articles of faith which cannot be seen to be
necessarily true. It means only that a principle is the kind of thing which is *capable*
of being seen to be necessarily true, whereas
an article of faith is the kind of thing which
is *incapable* of being seen to be necessarily
true.

To see this point clearly, let us contrast
the principle of non-contradiction with the
article of faith that Jesus is divine. As principle and as article of faith, respectively,

neither is derivable from other beliefs and
many other beliefs are derivable from each
of them; they are alike, that is to say, in
being both underivable and foundational.
In the case of the principle of non-contradiction, however, the very meanings of the
constituent terms require that the principle be true: "Being is being", "A particular
being is the particular being that it is", "A
thing cannot be other than it is", "A thing
cannot both have and not have a given
property at the some time and in the same
respect," etc. But this self-verification is
certainly not the case with the belief that
"Jesus is divine" or that "Jesus is God."
Here the meanings of the terms certainly
do not require the truth of the belief; it is
perfectly possible, semantically or logical-
ly, for Jesus not to be God. Indeed, rather
than the meanings of the terms requiring
the truth of the belief, here the very opposite might seem more likely to be the case.
Certainly not self-evident or necessarily
true, the proposition that "Jesus is God"
seems more likely to be self-evidently or
necessarily *false*, since it seems to identify

the finite with the infinite, the imperfect
with the perfect, etc. So Tertullian for one
understood it: "I believe because it's ab-
surd," he boasted. "What has Athens to do
with Jerusalem?"[4] What does logical necessity or analyticity have to do with the
Judaeo-Christian faith?

The logical or semantical status of principles is therefore quite unlike that of articles of faith, even though principles are
like articles of faith in being unprovable
and foundational. Principles can be seen
to be necessarily true by virtue of the
meanings of their terms, but articles of
faith cannot. Even if a principle is not seen
to be true self-evidencingly by virtue of
the meanings of its terms, however, it can
still be seen that the rejection of such a
foundation would cause the intelligibility
of the world to come crashing down on our
heads. "If we should be forced to realize
that nothing in our experience possesses
any stability," C. I. Lewis points out, "—
that our principle, 'Nothing can both be
and not be', was merely a verbalism, ap-
plying to nothing more than momentarily

—that denouement would rock our world
to its foundations."[5] Hence the foundational character of a principle is also a very
strong reason for believing in it, even if
it should not be seen to be self-evidently
true in itself. This is an important point
to which I will return later.

Thus principles cannot be abandoned
without intellectual suicide, while articles
of faith can be—even though it may be
that they *should* not be abandoned. If principles are rejected, life loses all intelligibility, meaning, and sense; we are then re-
duced to the vegetative state, as Aristotle
said.[6] Articles of faith, on the other hand,
may be rejected without the world's thereby losing its intelligibility, its meaning and
sense—although it may be the case, as we
shall see later, that if articles of faith are
rejected life loses *ultimate* meaning and
purpose.

Hence articles of faith may be abandoned, but rational principles cannot be.
This means that one *need* not accept any
belief other than ones of the rationalist's
three kinds: first order beliefs, second or-

der beliefs, and principles. There may also
be third order beliefs which are not principles, but if so these, if accepted, must be
accepted on faith; and if this is done, the
rationalist is to this extent no longer a pure
rationalist. But this *need* not be so. The
rationalist need not accept any third order
beliefs other than principles. Thus a pure
rationalism is possible—though only when
its meaning is seen to include principles as
well as first and second order beliefs. And
thus rationalism is vindicated, and Margenau's view is shown to be wrong. Reason
need not have recourse to faith.

Now, however, we must see that this
vindication of rationalism is also on its
own terms a vindication of religious belief
—or rather, as we shall see, a vindication
of certain kinds of religious belief. The
first and most important thing to under-
stand in order to see that this is true is that
some religious beliefs are rational as *first*
order beliefs, that is, as ostensible records
of immediate religious experience. Such
experience is usually called "mystical experience" or "direct revelation." This does

not mean, we must here again be remind-
ed, that such religious first order beliefs
are always or necessarily *true,* any more
than non-religious first order beliefs are
always true. A first order belief was defined, it will be remembered, as one which
seems to be a record of immediate experience; but such seeming may be a mere
seeming and the belief be actually false.
Moses' belief that God spoke to him from
the burning bush was a legitimate first order belief, although it might be the case
that it was false. Yet it was also a religious
belief because it was about God. Hence,
again, some religious beliefs are rational
as first order beliefs; and such religious beliefs must therefore be acceptable to the
rationalist if he is to be faithful to his position.

Here the rationalist might object that
such mystical experiences or immediate
revelations are not legitimate first order
beliefs on the ground that they purport or
attempt to record experiences which are
essentially inexpressible or ineffable. In re-
ply to this objection I do not here want to

go into the question of the extent to which
this allegation is true. I am inclined to
think that it is partially but not wholly true
that mystical experiences are inexpressible.
The only point I want to make now, however, is that to whatever extent this charge
is true against beliefs which seem to record mystical experiences or personal revelations it is also true to that same extent of
all first order beliefs. The reason for this
is simply the diversity which always exists
between immediate experience and expressions of it. This paper as it is immediately
experienced here and now by me with my
perceptual idiosyncrasies is certainly different from and not completely expressible
in the reports of it which I give to myself
and others, and this is no less true of my
experience of the paper than it is of Moses'
experience of God speaking from the burning bush. Hence my belief that this is paper before me is no more legitimate—and
only a lunatic would say that it's not legitimate—than Moses' belief that God is
speaking to him from a burning bush. The
two types of belief therefore stand or fall

together; they are equally legitimately rational—though of course not thereby necessarily true. Hence if the non-religious belief is rational as a first order belief, so is the religious belief. Hence, again, religious beliefs may be rational without ceasing to be religious.

At this point, however, the rationalist might again object—this time arguing that if religious beliefs are, by the above argument, rational, then by that very fact they cease to be religious, because it belongs to a religious belief to be non-rational. Religious beliefs are matters of faith, the rationalist thus objects; and that is, wholly or partly, what is meant by a belief's being religious. Surely, however, it is easy to see that this objection begs the whole question. All that is necessary is that there be some real distinction between religious and non-religious beliefs; it is not necessary that this distinction consist in the rationality of the latter and the non-rationality of the former. *That* distinction has now been shown to be mistaken, and all that we now need is some other legitimate distinction between the two kinds of belief. This distinction can easily be supplied in terms of the difference in the *objects* of the two kinds of belief. God is not the same as paper, so a belief about God is different from a belief about paper.

This particular distinction is of course not sufficiently general, since there are non-religious first order beliefs which are not about paper and there are religious first order beliefs which are not directly or primarily about God. But such a generalization of the difference between the objects of religious and the objects of non-religious first order beliefs can surely be made, at least in principle, even if any given generalized difference may be questionable. Let us say, for example, that a religious belief (and *a fortiori* a first order religious belief) is one whose object is, directly or indirectly, man's affective or effective relation to God. A non-religious belief is then simply any other belief, of whatever order. If someone should differ with this characterization of a religious belief, preferring to describe it as an expression of Tillich's "ultimate concern" or Schleiermacher's feeling of absolute dependence or whatever, I would not here have any quarrel with him. All I am concerned to point out here is that religious and non-religious beliefs may be distinguished in some legitimate way without the former thereby ceasing to be rational. Of course it should again be noted that religious beliefs, even if rational, are not thereby true, any more than non-religious ones are. But the important point here is that religious beliefs are, as religious, different from non-religious ones without any sacrifice of their rationality; and some of these religious beliefs are first order ones. Thus some religious beliefs are rational as first order beliefs—as much so as any non-religious first order belief.

Having laid this foundation we now need only to note that there are also rational *second* order religious beliefs, because from first order religious beliefs (or even from third order ones, as we shall see), we seem to be able to derive other religious beliefs by means of logical rules, just as we can derive non-religious second order beliefs. For example, from the first order religious belief that God himself personally gave Moses the ten commandments can apparently be derived the second order religious belief that the ten commandments should be obeyed by all the Israelites. Or, from the third order religious belief that Jesus is divine I seem to be able to derive the second order religious belief that I should follow his teachings. And so on. Different supplementary premises are of course needed in these religious cases than in non-religious ones, but so far as I can see the rules of inference which may legitimately be used in the two cases are the same—or at least they overlap. Of course the rules of inference employed in deriving second order religious beliefs presuppose principles, such as the principle of non-contradiction. But once again this is also true of non-religious second order beliefs, as we have seen. The important point in all this is that there are second order religious beliefs which are fully as rational as second order non-religious beliefs are.

III

Religious beliefs have thus been vindicated as rational, for the logic of religious beliefs may be exactly the same as the logic of non-religious beliefs with only their objects being different. Beliefs having to do with man's affective or effective relation to God—or with whatever else is taken to be the religious object—may be just like beliefs about anything else in the world. The rationality of such religious beliefs does of course presuppose the consistency of, or absence of contradiction in, the religious idea or object, whatever that may be decided to be. But this is also true of non-religious beliefs: their rationality also presupposes the consistency of, or absence of contradiction in, their objects. Hence once again religious and non-religious beliefs stand or fall together. If their objects are coherent, then they may be equally rational—either as first order beliefs or as second order beliefs derivable from first order ones.

However, this rationality of religious beliefs does require (in addition to prin-

ciples) the presence of first order religious
beliefs and thus the presence of immediate
religious experience. A belief may be a
second order religious belief in the sense
that it has a religious object and is derivable from other accepted religious beliefs,
but if one or more of these other beliefs
is neither a first order belief nor a principle—neither a record of immediate religious experience nor a third order belief
which can be seen to be true in itself—
then such a second order religious belief
is not fully rational. It is rationally derived,
but its foundation is not rational in either
of the two required senses: either as a first
order belief or as a principle. Thus, again,
the rationality of religious belief requires
immediate religious experience. But this is
just exactly what is so often lacking and
unavailable to the believer. Indeed, people
whose religious beliefs are adequately
based upon their own immediate religious
experiences surely constitute a very small
minority of the total number of religious
believers—at least in the history of the
western world. And when first order reli-

gious beliefs, and thus immediate religious experiences, are lacking, then the believer can derive his second order religious beliefs only from third order religious beliefs. And these, as we have seen, are not principles (or at least most of them are not); their truth is not guaranteed by the meanings of their terms. Such foundational religious beliefs, then, must be articles of faith.

Here finally arises, then, the crucial problem: Can there be any *reason* at all for accepting something on faith? Can it ever be *rational* to accept an article of faith? And if so, how?

It is clear by the very nature of the case that there cannot be any reason for accepting an article of faith in the standard senses of "reason" which we have been talking about. This is so simply because, as we have seen, articles of faith are not principles, they are not first order beliefs, and they are not second order beliefs which follow from first order beliefs. Or, to put the matter more obviously tautologically, there cannot be any reason in our rational-

ist's sense of reason for accepting an article
of faith because if there were it would then
be a rational belief, albeit a religious one,
and not an article of *faith* at all. Hence if
there is to be any reason for accepting
something on faith, it must be a reason
in a broader and looser sense than any
given to that term by our rationalist — a
broader sense perhaps better expressed by
the word "justification" than by the word
"reason." Furthermore, any such reason or
justification for accepting an article of
faith must somehow lie within the context
of faith itself, since we have seen that we
cannot justify accepting an article of faith
by means of any consideration which falls
properly within the context of reason, as
the rationalist conceives reason. And this
conclusion seems to be confirmed by the
traditional view that there is no merit in
the believer's faith if it is accepted only
for some external, extraneous reason. But
what is there within the context of faith
which could be a reason or justification for
accepting an article of faith? How can the

nature of faith itself provide a reason for
its own acceptibility?

In the first place, we should be remind-
ed that an article of faith does *not* provide
a reason for its own acceptibility by being
self-justifying, simply as an isolated proposition, as a rational principle does—for instance, the principle of non-contradiction.
A principle is self-justifying, we saw, because it may be seen to be self-evidently or
necessarily true, its truth being guaranteed
by the very meanings of its terms without
reference to anything beyond it. Of course
this is sometimes not seen to be so, but it
always *can* be. But an article of faith—
for example, the belief that Jesus is divine
—is the sort of thing, we also saw, that is
not capable of being seen to be self-evidently or necessarily true, just by virtue of
the meanings of its terms, taken just in itself without reference to anything beyond
it. Hence articles of faith are not self-justifying, not self-evidencingly or semantically
true simply as propositions taken in themselves without reference to anything beyond them, as principles are. So how then

can the very nature of faith provide a justification for its acceptance?

The answer to this question which I
would like to suggest can be brought out
by remembering the ways in which articles
of faith are like rational principles, and
with that by broadening our view from
articles of faith taken just as isolated propositions to the total logical context of faith
in which articles of faith appear. Even
though articles of faith are quite unlike
rational principles by virtue of the fact
that the latter are capable of being seen
to be necessarily true whereas the former
are not, as we have just again seen, still
articles of faith are like rational principles
in being *foundational* and *underivable*.
Each is underivable simply because each
is a third order belief. Neither an article
of faith nor a rational principle, that is to
say, is either a putative report of immediate experience or something which follows
from any such report by logical rules.
More importantly, however, articles of
faith are like rational principles in being
foundational; each is an underivable

foundation upon which other beliefs (second order beliefs) are founded, or from which these other beliefs are derived. It is true, of course, that articles of faith are foundational in a different way than principles are, as we also saw, for rational principles cannot be abandoned without intellectual suicide, and this is not true of articles of faith. Perhaps they shouldn't be abandoned, but they can be. Although articles of faith are thus not foundational in exactly the same way that rational principles are, however, their foundational characters, are *analogous*. And this, finally, is the key to understanding the way in which belief in articles of faith may be justified.

Let me first put the analogy this way: Without *principles* life has no *sense;* without *faith* life has no *meaning* or *purpose.* Without principles the world would be unintelligible; without faith the world is pointless. Or, again, this analogy between the foundational character of articles of faith and that of rational principles comes out nicely in the word "impossible": With-

out principles life is impossible (literally
or conceptually); without *faith* life is "im-
*poss*ible!" (figuratively or morally). Or,
finally, this analogy between faith and
principle may also be fittingly expressed
by exploiting the ambiguity—which is by
no means a total equivocation—contained
in the word "meaningless": Without principles life is meaningless; without faith
life is meaningless. Without principles life
is meaningless in the way that the Jabber-
wocky Song in *Through the Looking Glass*
is (until its words are assigned meanings)
—" 'Twas brillig, and the slithy toves/ Did
gyre and gimble in the wabe . . ." Without faith life is meaningless in the way
that it was for Ecclesiastes, the Preacher
—"Vanity of vanities, all is vanity!" The
word "meaningless" is indeed used somewhat differently in these two cases, but
I submit that we do not have here two
completely different meanings or uses of
the word. Rather these uses are analogous;
they share a common core of meaning differently applied. Articles of faith are not
the same as rational principles, nor is the

foundational character of faith identical
with that of principles. But they *are analogous*: as principles stand in relation to
intelligibility, so faith stands in relation to
purpose, point, or meaning.

Belief in articles of faith may thus be
seen to be justifiable or reasonable in a
way which is analogous to, though different from, the second of the two ways in
which belief in rational principles is justifiable or rational—by virtue, that is, of their
foundational character. In this sense there
can be a reason, a justification, for accepting something on faith—namely, whenever
such acceptance on faith is seen to be a
necessary condition for one's life to have
meaning, point, or purpose. Of course this
is not a strictly rational justification in the
sense in which I have been using the term
"rational," for we have seen that there can
by definition be no strictly rational reason
or justification for accepting something on
faith. It is always possible to ask meaning-
fully: "Why *shouldn't* life be meaningless,
"impossible," purposeless? What rational
evidence is there for the belief that life

and the world *have* meaning, point, and purpose?" Although this is not a strictly rationally compelling reason, therefore, I believe that it is entirely *analogous* to a strictly rationally compelling reason—or at least that it may be for many people and that in fact it probably is for most of those who accept a faith. Why may I reasonably believe the Christian story, for instance? Because it gives life and the world a meaning and point which they otherwise lack. This reason, which is the foundational character of faith, seems entirely analogous to the foundational character of rational principles as a reason for accepting them. Why must I believe that there are stable meanings, for example? Because if that were not so, I would be unable to speak, or even to think. It is of course true that many people reject faith in the Christian story. But it is also true that some people—Cratylus, for instance—have rejected the principle that there are stable meanings. This fact does not make us think that we are not justified in accepting that principle, however. And in like fashion the fact that many people reject the Christian faith should not make us think we are not justified in accepting it.

So it is, I suggest, that there may be a justification, a reason in a somewhat relaxed sense of that word, for accepting something on faith, since the foundational character of an article of faith is analogous to the foundational character of a rational principle. Such reasonableness of faith, such justification for accepting an article of faith, does not mean that that article of faith is thereby true, however. Here again faith is exactly parallel to reason. In both cases accepting the belief *does* mean accepting the belief *as* true, of course; to believe a proposition is to believe that it is true. But this does not imply that the belief which is accepted or the proposition which is believed is in fact *really* true; it may actually be false. We saw before that the rationality of accepting a first or second order belief or a principle does not imply that any of those accepted beliefs is true. A belief which it is rational to accept and irrational to reject—such as that there will be too many Ph.D.'s during the next ten years—may still be false. In like manner the reasonableness or justifiability of accepting an article of faith *as* true does not imply that that accepted article of faith *is* true. It may be reasonable to believe that the world has a purpose even though that belief may in fact be false. Thus it is the reasonableness or justifiability of faith which I am talking about, not the truth or falsity of the belief which is accepted on faith.

Moreover, in talking about the reasonableness of believing—be it a rational belief or an article of faith—I am not quite talking about *motives* for believing or *causes* of actually believing something. That is, I am talking about the logic of belief (in the broad sense of "logic") rather than about the psychology of belief. If a person believes that it is reasonable or justifiable to accept a certain belief, then that fact does indeed usually incline him in the direction of accepting that belief, since most people are reasonable; and it sometimes causes him actually to accept it. However, as we all know, it is too often the case that we do not accept a belief even though it seems reasonable for us to do so, and it is also too often the case that we accept a belief even though it seems unreasonable for us to do so. But this just means that people are not always reasonable, that they sometimes—perhaps usually—believe something because of their emotions or passions; and that comes as no surprise. Yet people ought to be reasonable even if they're not.

It is just precisely here that the view I am suggesting differs from Blaise Pascal's famous religious wager[7] and William James' very similar and equally famous "will to believe."[8] Both Pascal and James held that religious beliefs are totally beyond the bounds of reason, and they therefore had to offer a non-rational justification for accepting religious beliefs—the believer's happiness, in the case of Pascal, and the demands of the believer's "passional nature," in the case of James. The view I am suggesting comes closer to making the justification for accepting

articles of faith a matter of reason rather
than of passion, though of course it does
so by stretching "reason" or "reasonableness" to cover somewhat more than it does
in the rationalism of the rational man I
have described. My view, that is to say,
makes it reasonable, if not narrowly rational, to accept an article of faith, for my
view claims that the foundational character of an article of faith is analogous to
the foundational character of a rational
principle. And even the rationalist will
allow that the foundational character of
a rational principle is a good reason for
accepting that principle. By reason of
parity, therefore, the foundational character of an article of faith should likewise
be admitted to be a good reason for accepting that faith.

To conclude this lecture I want to put
this last point somewhat differently. That
life should be meaningful, that the world
should have point and purpose, seems to
me to be an intellectual matter, whether
or not it is also an emotional or hedonic
one. A faith that life and the world are

meaningful may indeed increase one's happiness or satisfy certain of one's emotional needs; and this fact may, in some people, be an effective cause of their accepting that faith. In addition to this, however, there is the cognitive sense that life and the world make when that faith is accepted; and this is a matter of the head rather than of the heart or belly. Whether or not such a faith increases one's happiness or satisfies one's passional nature, therefore, reason too, in a broadened sense of reason, says that such a faith is reasonable and justifiable. The mind's eye then sees a more meaningful world.

NOTES

1. Henry Margenau, *The New Faith of Science*, Northfield, Minn.: Carleton College, 1953, pp. 9-10.

2. The view that there is an experience or intuition of being has been defended perhaps most notably by Jacques Maritain, especially in his *A Preface to Metaphysics* (New York: Sheed and Ward, 1939). An interesting defense of this view is given by Stanford K. Pritchard in his "Metaphysics and the Metaphysical experience," *International Philosophical Quarterly*, Vol. VI, No. 2 (June, 1966), pp. 214-229; and Pritchard here also discusses the views of Maritain, Heidegger, and others on this question.

3. For example in my essay "Insight," Chapter I of *Patterns of the Life World* (edited by James Edie, Francis H. Parker, and Calvin O. Schrag), Evanston: Northwestern University Press, 1970.

4. Tertullian, *On Prescription Against Heretics*, Chapter 7.

5. C. I. Lewis, *Mind and the World Order*, New York: Charles Scribner's Sons, 1929, p. 306.

6. Aristotle, *Metaphysics*, Bk. IV, Ch. 4, 1006a 14-15.

7. Blaise Pascal, *Thoughts*, number 233.

8. William James, *The Will to Believe, and Other Essays on Popular Philosophy*, New York: Longmans, Green and Company, 1917, pp. 1-31.

The Aquinas Lectures

Published by the Marquette University Press
Milwaukee, Wisconsin 53233

Humanism and Theology (1943) by Werner Jaeger, Ph.D., Litt.D., (1888-1961) University professor, Harvard University. sBN 87462-107-0

The Nature and Origins of Scientism (1944) by John Wellmuth. sBN 87462-108-9

Cicero in the Courtroom of St. Thomas Aquinas (1945) by E. K. Rand, Ph.D., Litt.D., LL.D., (1871-1945) Pope professor of Latin, *emeritus,* Harvard University. sBN 87462-109-7

St. Thomas and Epistemology (1946) by Louis-Marie Regis, O.P., Th.L., Ph.D., director of the Albert the Great Institute of Mediaeval Studies, University of Montreal.
sBN 87462-110-0

St. Thomas and the Greek Moralists (1947, Spring) by Vernon J. Bourke, Ph.D., professor of philosophy, St. Louis University, St. Louis, Missouri. sBN 87462-111-9

History of Philosophy and Philosophical Education (1947, Fall) by Étienne Gilson of the *Académie française,* director of studies and professor of the history of Mediaeval philosophy, Pontifical Institute of Mediaeval Studies, Toronto. sBN 87462-112-7

The Natural Desire for God (1948) by William R. O'Connor, S.T.L., Ph.D., former professor of dogmatic theology, St. Joseph's Seminary, Dunwoodie, N.Y. sBN 87462-113-5

St. Thomas and the World State (1949) by Robert M. Hutchins, former Chancellor of the University of Chicago, president of the Fund for the Republic. <small>SBN 87462-114-3</small>

Method in Metaphysics (1950) by Robert J. Henle, S.J., Ph.D., academic vice-president, St. Louis University, St. Louis, Missouri. <small>SBN 87462-115-1</small>

Wisdom and Love in St. Thomas Aquinas (1951) by Étienne Gilson of the *Académie française*, director of studies and professor of the history of Mediaeval philosophy, Pontifical Institute of Mediaeval Studies, Toronto. <small>SBN 87462-116-X</small>

The Good in Existential Metaphysics (1952) by Elizabeth G. Salmon, Ph.D., professor of philosophy in the graduate school, Fordham University. <small>SBN 87462-117-8</small>

St. Thomas and the Object of Geometry (1953) by Vincent Edward Smith, Ph.D., director, Philosophy of Science Institute, St. John's University. <small>SBN 87462-118-6</small>

Realism and Nominalism Revisited (1954) by Henry Veatch, Ph.D., professor and chairman of the department of philosophy, Northwestern University. <small>SBN 87462-119-4</small>

Imprudence in St. Thomas Aquinas (1955) by Charles J. O'Neil, Ph.D., professor of philosophy, Villanova University. <small>SBN 87462-120-8</small>

The Truth That Frees (1956) by Gerard Smith, S.J., Ph.D., professor of philosophy, Marquette University.   sBN 87462-121-6

St. Thomas and the Future of Metaphysics (1957) by Joseph Owens, C.Ss.R., Ph.D., professor of philosophy, Pontifical Institute of Mediaeval Studies, Toronto.   sBN 87462-122-4

Thomas and the Physics of 1958: A Confrontation (1958) by Henry Margenau, Ph.D., Eugene Higgins professor of physics and natural philosophy, Yale University.
    sBN 87462-123-2

Metaphysics and Ideology (1959) by Wm. Oliver Martin, Ph.D., professor of philosophy, University of Rhode Island.   sBN 87462-124-0

Language, Truth and Poetry (1960) by Victor M. Hamm, Ph.D., professor of English, Marquette University.   sBN 87462-125-9

Metaphysics and Historicity (1961) by Emil L. Fackenheim, Ph.D., professor of philosophy, University of Toronto.   sBN 87462-126-7

The Lure of Wisdom (1962) by James D. Collins, Ph.D., professor of philosophy, St. Louis University.   sBN 87462-127-5

Religion and Art (1963) by Paul Weiss, Ph.D. Sterling professor of philosophy, Yale University.   sBN 87462-128-3

St. Thomas and Philosophy (1964) by Anton C. Pegis, Ph.D., professor of philosophy, Pontifical Institute of Mediaeval Studies, Toronto.
SBN 87462-129-1

The University In Process (1965) by John O. Riedl, Ph.D., dean of faculty, Queensboro Community College.
SBN 87462-130-5

The Pragmatic Meaning of God (1966) by Robert O. Johann, associate professor of philosophy, Fordham University.
SBN 87462-131-3

Religion and Empiricism (1967) by John E. Smith, Ph.D., professor of philosophy, Yale University.
SBN 87462-132-1

The Subject (1968) by Bernard Lonergan, S.J., S.T.D., professor of Dogmatic Theory, Regis College, Ontario and Gregorian University, Rome.
SBN 87462-133-X

Beyond Trinity (1969) by Bernard J. Cooke, S.T.D.
SBN 87462-134-8

Ideas and Concepts (1970) by Julius R. Weinberg, Ph.D., Vilas Professor of Philosophy, University of Wisconsin.
SBN 87462-135-6

Reason and Faith Revisited (1971) by Francis H. Parker, Ph.D., head of the philosophy department, Purdue University, Lafayette, Indiana.
SBN 87462-136-4

Uniform format, cover and binding.